Putting the Boat to Bed

Poems by
Deirdre Foster

Illustrations by
Nikki Foster

First published 2018 by IRON Press
5 Marden Terrace
Cullercoats
North Shields
NE30 4PD
tel/fax +44(0)191 2531901
ironpress@xlnmail.com
www.ironpress.co.uk

ISBN 978-0-9954579-5-9
Printed by Field Print, Boldon on Tyne

Poems © Deirdre Foster 2018
Illustrations © Nikki Foster 2018
This edition © IRON Press 2018

Cover and book design Kate Jones and Peter Mortimer
Cover drawing © Nikki Foster
Typeset in Garamond

IRON Press books are distributed by NBN International
and represented by Inpress Ltd
Churchill House, 12 Mosley Street,
Newcastle upon Tyne, NE1 1DE
tel: +44(0)191 2308104
www.inpressbooks.co.uk

To Eppie

DEIRDRE FOSTER was born in Sydney, Australia and moved as a child to South-West England. A road accident cut short a dancing career and Deirdre moved back to Australia to work with indigenous Australian people in the outback. She returned to the UK where she married and brought up her children. Deirdre bases her life in and around the varied landscapes of the South-West.

NIKKI FOSTER was born in Poole in 1984. In her late teens she left Dorset for London and studied Painting at Camberwell College of Arts. After ten years in London studying and later working for the National Portrait Gallery, Nikki relocated to Dublin with her partner and two children. She is a freelance portrait artist and illustrator and has worked on several editorial projects.

The Poems

Drugs Den	6
The Drowning	8
1 Year Old Child	10
Visit from the Daughter	12
Instructions for a Dancer Circa 1970	14
The Commute	16
Seizure	18
The Match	20
House Clearance	22
Murder House	24
Letter to a Grandchild Departing Overseas	26
Somerset Winter	28
Putting the Boat to Bed	30

Drugs Den

I rarely see the drug takers,
They dart occasionally
From door to bicycle with mobile phones,
At odd times of the day and night.

We share some common spaces
Entrances, exits, party walls,
Drives and straying plants.
The cat remains a joint possession.

Their garden is a natural wilderness,
It supports all types of plants.
Mine is ordered and geometrical,
There are plants with long names
And a neat patio.

These people have the looks,
The expression, an air of guilty uncertainty.
I want to reach out, catch the fleeting figures,
But doubt our worlds will ever collide.

Living on the edge, patrolling the borderline.
It's not long before they leave.
The tattered white sheet still hangs
In the window.

The Drowning

The sea is flat tonight,
Its still exterior
Shall enter
My turbulent interior.

There is a sea wall
From which
A twisted iron ladder
Digs deep
Into the calm water.

One step at a time.
It will only cause
A slight ripple
In this vast bay.

The sea is flat, tonight.
Now tomorrow,
Tomorrow, there might be a storm.

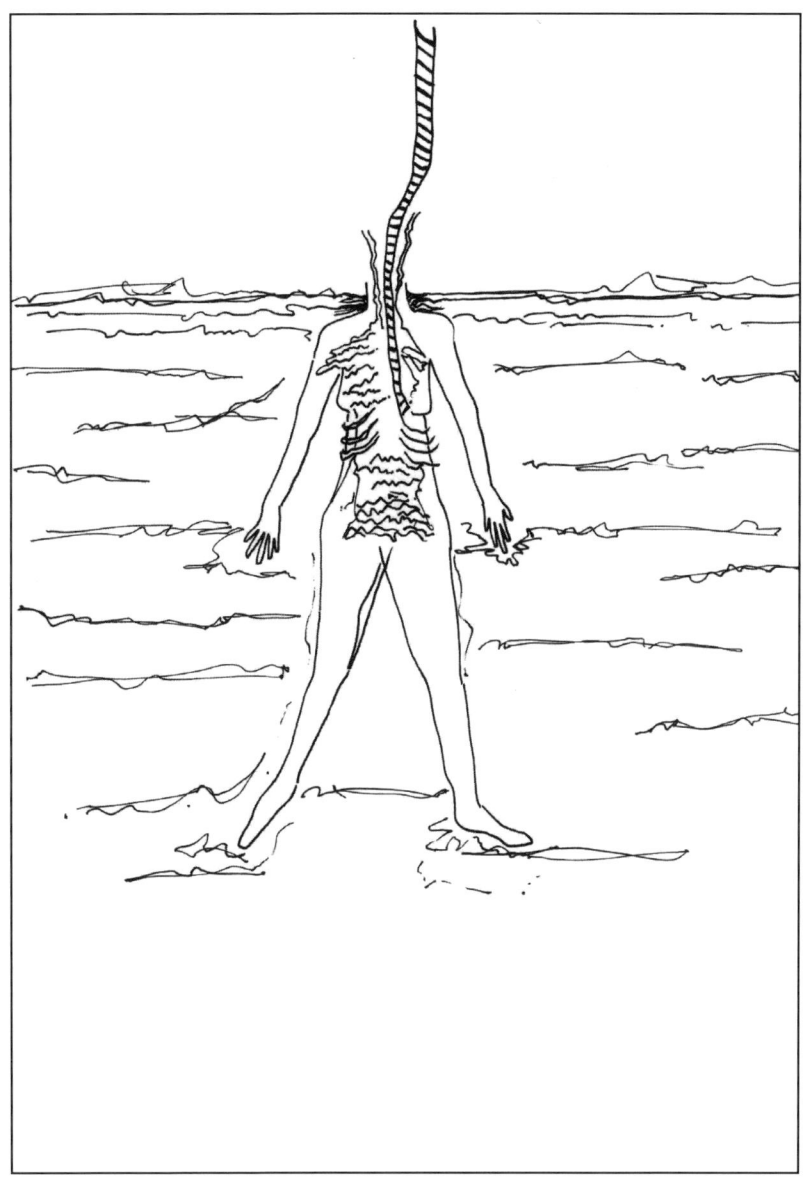

1 year old Child

I need to complete this blank canvas quickly.

Shall I paint you with
an aggressive stance,
hands on hips,
looking beyond,
above the horizon.

Dynamic rainbow colours,
challenging eyes,
direct, hard, enquiring.
I am indecisive.
I could use pastel shades,
a meek stance,
curling, bowing away from the light,
floating over the canvas,
in a wash of pale hues.

I assemble my brushes
turn around
and you have begun
painting yourself.

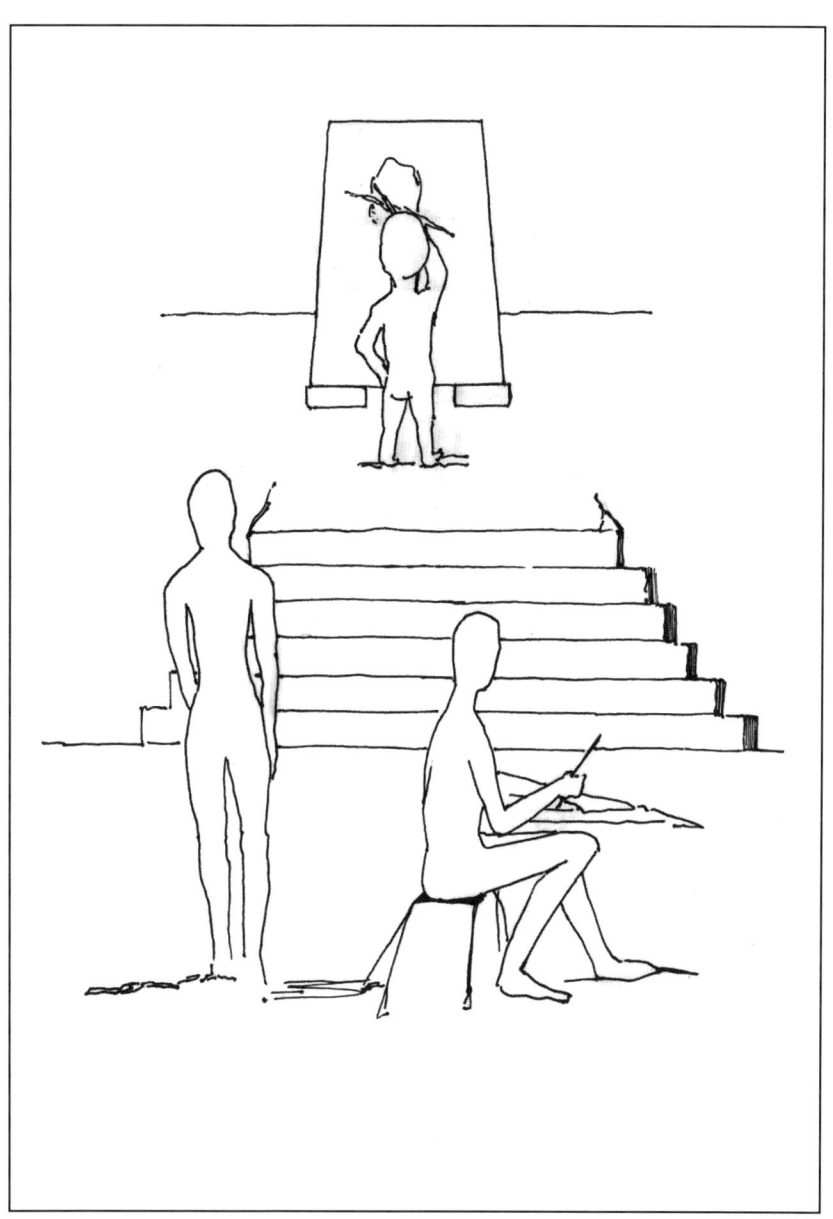

Visit from the Daughter

A hurricane bolted through
The house.
An express train made
An emergency stop.

Burglar-proof locks
Are checked.
Sell-by-date food discarded.
Plugs are pulled
From sockets.
Cats dash for cover,
Behind,
Under, on top of
Any spare seat.

'See you in the spring,'
She said.
'We'll do a spring clean.'
The dog
Wags its tail,
Chewing on the last skeletal remains
Of the visit.

Instructions for Dancer Circa 1970

The life I didn't have
Is often seen
On art gallery walls
Landscaped mystical gardens

Dancers curl
Huddle in baggy jumpers
Rest
In those musical interludes
They look poised
Clutch cold coffee
In white plastic cups
Stalking horses
Ready to jump into action
Catch the time slot
For each particular move

When the studio door closes
The white chalk dust will smudge
The scraps of notation scribble
Will litter the floor
Next day
Next millennium
The dance will reinvent itself

The Commute

Coming away
From where I've just been
Leaving behind
The people, places I know
Travelling to
The familiar faces
From the familiar faces
Watching the forest
Evolving, recovering, renewing
The train halts
Leaves on the line
Odd announcements and apologies
Whistle through the carriages
I should be
Complaining about the journey
The never-ending commute
This is my time
This is my journey

Seizure

Time lies stranded
On the shores of understanding
Or should I say misunderstanding?
They assured me it happened
There in the street
Or was it in the bar maybe?
Even on the sands, at the shops
I'm waiting to hear what happened
But memory like time is stranded
And no-one as yet has filled me in
On those all-important details.

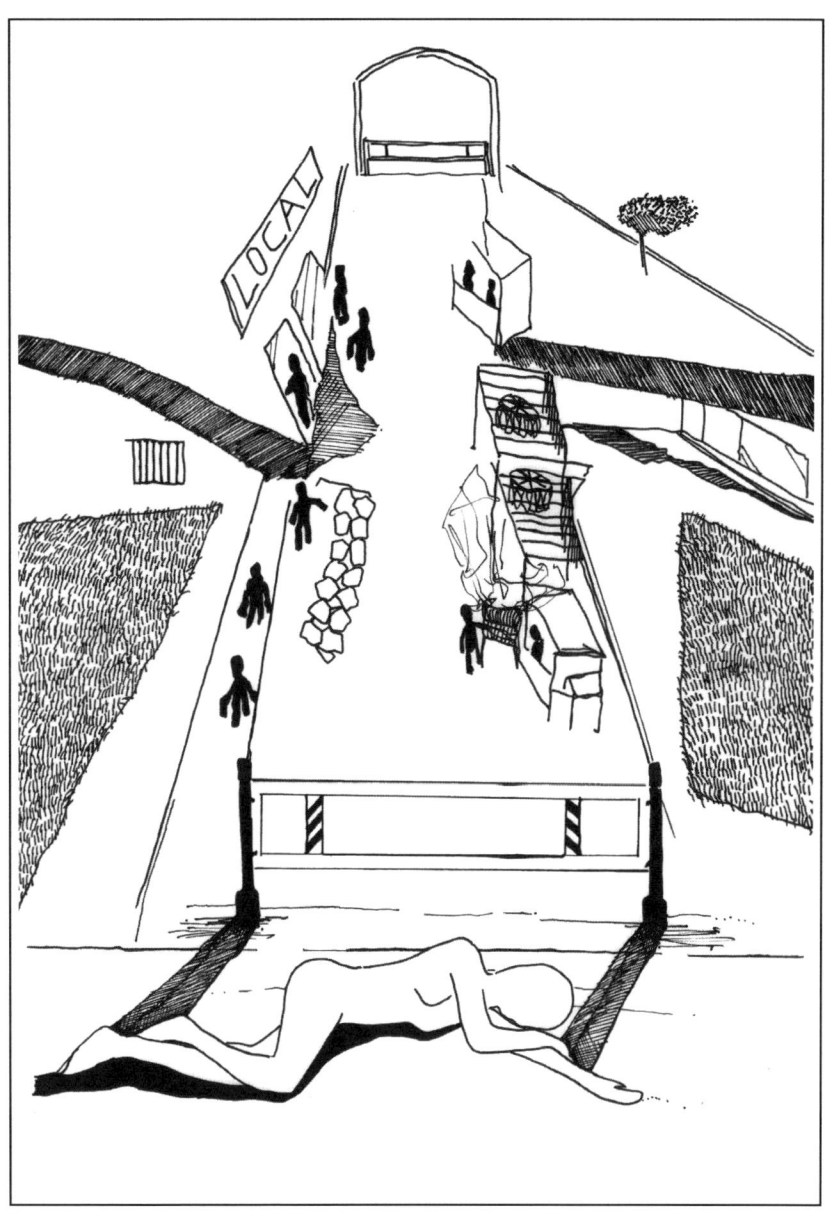

The Match

In the dark gentle gathering
Of ladies who lunch
We all heard the woman
No-one made eye contact
"It was a perfect marriage.
It was always such fun!"

For most of us
Fun was the occasional bonus
And perfection
Not even in the vocabulary

It was almost a biblical story
The quiet glowing woman
It was a story
In which we all wanted
To play a part

House Clearance

I was given the task
Of mapping your last dreams
I could reassemble
The bookcase
That was never screwed
To the wall
Carefully finish sticking
The Broderie Anglaise
It's the dream itself
That I have yet to locate
Without that
The map is useless
I have called in the experts
To clear the house

Murder House

A child's football
Kicked over the wall
Into the neglected long grass
No-one has dared
Retrieve that ball

I heard she was a cheerful woman
Would have thrown back the ball
A nurse, they say
Maybe joined in the game

We crept over the grass
The dog and me
Leaving ghost footprints
I threw the ball
Back to the neighbour's garden
It left a shadow in the grass

Life has to go on
It has its patterns
The nurse would have wanted the children to play
Play football in the garden

Letter to a Grandchild Departing Overseas

We are still in the foothills
Of this friendship
You and I
We sometimes take the wrong track
Miss the turning
Food flies across the room
A favourite toy goes astray
I become lost in you
A child again
You search in vain for the mother
We need a mobile app
To find base camp
There we can swap stories
With the many others
I packed the correct kit
For this journey
Ready to ascend the summit
Only to find you have already left

Somerset Winter

Have you walked in waders
In your drowned world
Amongst the mallard ducks
Swimming in fields
Looking for their rivers?

Have you seen the discarded white plastic bags
Floating past the debris of torn trees
Imagining they are swans
Blown off course by the ferocious winds?

Have you turned the page?
It is now yesterday's news
As the waters slowly recede

I see you are not the grandfather
Lost on the levels
Trying to locate the spot
It was a farm
For the grandson to inherit
It was not a page in the story
It was the book

Putting the Boat to Bed

Didn't we have a great time
That last summer?
The wind was a gentle breeze
Coming from the best direction
South South-West
It got us there
Behind the islands
In the lee of the land
Water lapping the boat
The beer was plentiful
We could even swim
And the sun
Beat down

It was the others who went out that day
Who were caught by the changing tides
The sudden squalls
The onset of rain, wind
And the cold beat for home

IRON Press is among the country's longest
established independent literary publishers.
The press began operations in 1973 with
IRON Magazine which ran for 83 editions until 1997.
Since 1975 we have also brought out a regular list
of individual collections of poetry, fiction and drama
plus various anthologies ranging from *The Poetry of
Perestroika*, through *Limerick Nation*,
100 Island Poems and *Cold Iron, Ghost Stories
from the 21st Century*.

The press is one of the leading independent publishers
of haiku in the UK. Since 2013 we have also run
a regular IRON Press Festival round the harbour
in our native Cullercoats. *IRON in the Soul*,
our third festival, took place in Summer 2017.
Plans are afoot for a fourth festival in Summer 2019.

We are delighted to be a part of Inpress Ltd, which
was set up by Arts Council England to support
independent literary publishers.

Go to our website (www.ironpress.co.uk)
for full details of our titles and activities.